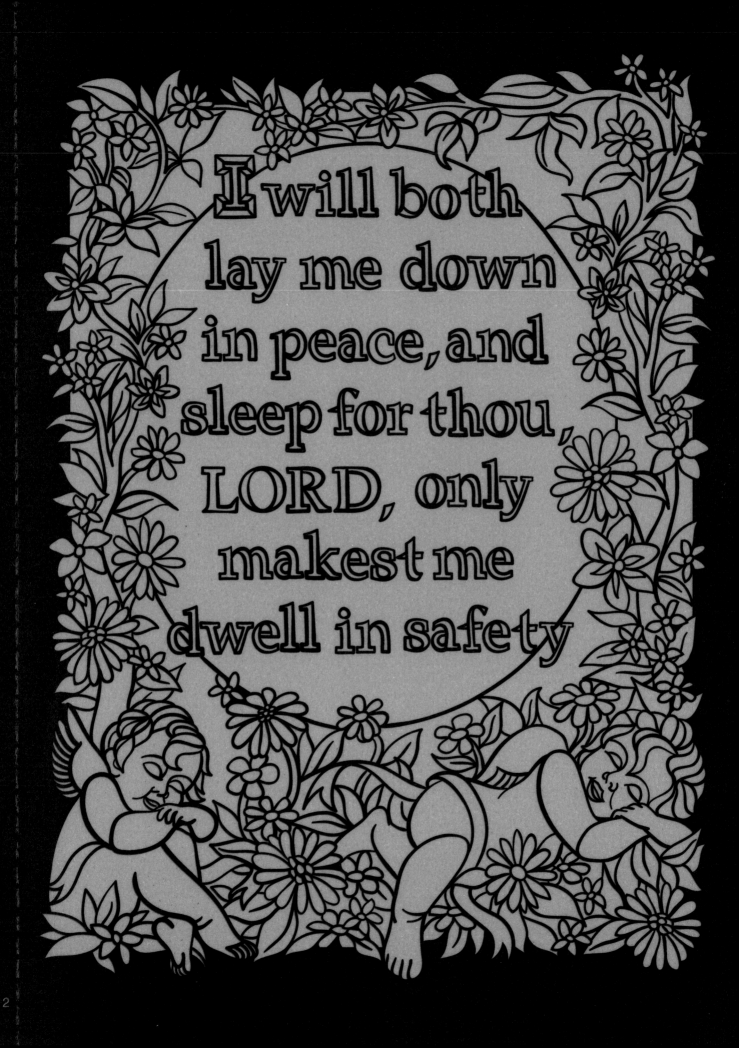

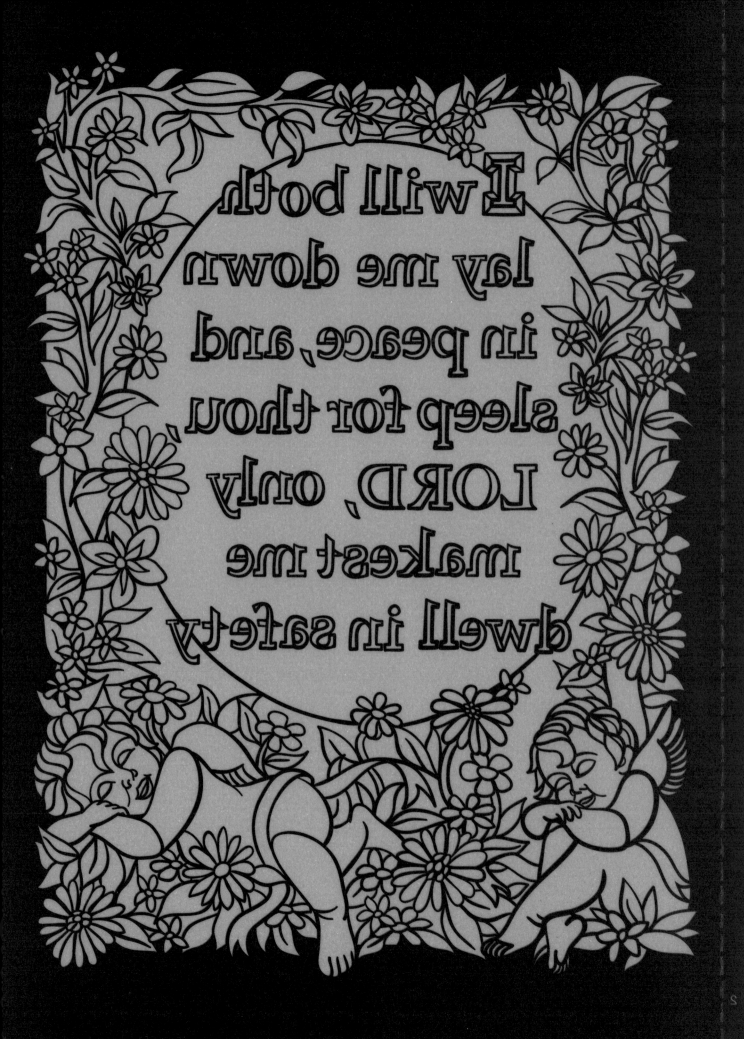

He maketh me
to lie down in
green pastures

He leadeth me
beside the
still waters

4

SAVE ME
FROM THE
LION'S MOUTH
FOR THOU HAST
HEARD ME FROM
THE HORNS OF
UNICORNS

SAVE ME
FROM THE
LIONS MOUTH

FOR THOU HAST
HEARD ME FROM
THE HORNS OF
UNICORNS

For with thee is the
fountain of life
In thy light shall
we see light

For thou wilt light my candle The LORD my God will enlighten my darkness

For thou wilt
light my candle
The LORD my
God will enlighten
my darkness

The Lord is my light
and my salvation
whom shall I fear

But the meek shall inherit the earth and delight themselves in the abundance of peace

But the meek
shall inherit the
earth and delight
themselves in
the abundance
of peace

The voice of the LORD is upon the waters